Hamsters

Alvin & Virginia Silverstein
Hamsters
All About Them

with photographs by Frederick Breda

Lothrop, Lee & Shepard Co./New York

ACKNOWLEDGMENTS

The authors would like to thank Frederick and Dorothy Breda and their son Fred for their enthusiastic support; Drs. Hulda Magalhaes and George Yerganian for their kind help and interest in the project; Bob, Glenn, Carrie, Sharon, Laura, and Kevin for their patient hours; and, of course, Betty, who gave birth just in time, Charlotte, Christie, Pierre, and the rest of the furry crew—especially Tom and his harem, whom we will never forget.

Printed in the United States of America.

1 2 3 4 5 78 77 76 75 74

Library of Congress Cataloging in Publication Data
Silverstein, Alvin.
   Hamsters.

   SUMMARY: A manual on the care, feeding, and breeding of golden hamsters as pets, with information on their life in the wild, their use in the lab, and other kinds of hamsters.
   1. Hamsters—Juvenile literature. [1. Hamsters]
I. Silverstein, Virginia B., joint author. II. Breda, Frederick, illus.
III. Title.
SF459.H3S54   636'.93'234   74-8863
ISBN 0-688-40056-6
ISBN 0-688-50056-0 (lib. bdg.)

FOR STEVEN BORMAN

Photographs in this book have been provided through the courtesy of the following:

Pages 10, 18 top, 24, 84: Charles River Lakeview, Newfield, N.J. 08344.

Pages 13, 41 bottom: Dr. George Yerganian.

Pages 14, 44 top, 45 bottom, 46, 68 bottom, 76 bottom: Alvin and Virginia Silverstein.

Page 31: H. Reinhard, Bruce Coleman, Inc.

Page 32: From *Mammals of the World* by Ernest P. Walker, copyright © The Johns Hopkins University Press.

Page 35: Jane Burton, Bruce Coleman, Inc.

Page 36: W. Jöchle, courtesy of G. Yerganian.

Pages 41 top, 57 center and bottom, 88, 111, 112: Reprinted by permission from *The Golden Hamster: Its Biology and Use in Medical Research* by Roger A. Hoffman, Paul F. Robinson, Hulda Magalhaes, editors, copyright © 1968 by Iowa State University Press, Ames, Iowa.

Pages 50, 53 top, 54 bottom, 59, 62, 113: Dr. Hulda Magalhaes.

Page 115 left and right: Dr. Paul H. Keyes.

Page 122: Dr. Walter J. Levy, Jr.

Contents

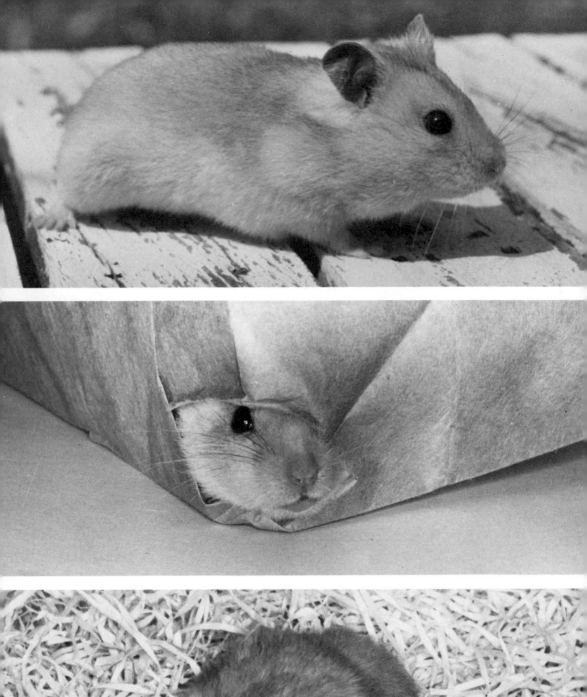

About Hamsters

Today millions of people have pet hamsters. These small animals can also be found in laboratories all over the world. It seems as though hamsters have always been a part of our lives. Yet their story really began quite recently, in 1930.

At the Hebrew University in Jerusalem, a medical researcher named Saul Adler had a problem. He was studying a tropical disease called kala-azar. In his research he was using small, mouselike animals called Chinese hamsters, hoping to find a cure that would save the lives of many human beings. But there were difficulties. At that time, no one knew how to get these small rodents to breed in the laboratory. Whenever new hamsters were needed for Dr. Adler's experiments, they had

to be trapped in China and shipped to Palestine. Sometimes Dr. Adler had to stop his experiments and wait
for a new shipment from the Far East. But he had heard
that small gray hamsters, very much like the Chinese
hamsters, could be found in Syria. And when he
learned, in 1930, that a zoologist friend of his, Israel
Aharoni, was going to Syria on a field trip, Dr. Adler was
delighted. If Professor Aharoni could bring back some
of the Syrian gray hamsters, the hamster supply problem
would be solved.

Professor Aharoni set out with his wife on a leisurely
trip through Syria, studying the animals of the area. On
the way, they caught a number of the gray hamsters. But

then they heard about a different kind of hamster, found only in the area around the city of Aleppo. These Syrian hamsters had reddish golden fur. Perhaps they, too, would be interesting and useful laboratory animals. So Professor Aharoni sent his interpreter to speak to the sheik of a village near Aleppo. The sheik called a meeting of the men of the village, and they decided to help. A group of them went out to a wheat field where the golden hamsters had been seen. They began to dig up

the field. At last they found what they were looking for
—a nest with a mother hamster and her litter of eleven
babies, curled up for their daytime sleep.

Soon the Aharonis were on their way back to Jerusalem with the gray hamsters they had collected and ten
of the baby golden hamsters. They left the gray hamsters
with Dr. Adler's group at the university and took the
little golden hamsters home with them. The scientists
at the university immediately tried to breed the gray
hamsters. But the males and females just fought viciously whenever they were put together. Soon the researchers gave up their attempt. If they had only been a
little more patient, the history of hamsters would have

12

been very different. Twenty years later it was found that wild gray hamsters breed very well in the laboratory if they are given a few months to get used to their new surroundings first. Now colonies of them are thriving in a number of laboratories throughout the world. But in 1930 no one realized this was possible. It seemed that Dr. Adler's experiments were doomed to failure—he would never have a reliable supply of gray hamsters.

Meanwhile, the Aharonis were busy playing foster parents to ten little golden hamsters. The babies were thriving on a diet of wheat stalks and grains, barley, bread, beans, cucumbers, nuts, and meat. They grew sleek and healthy, and so lively that they charmed everyone who saw them. Mrs. Aharoni took over the task of caring for them. She was so conscientious that some nights she hardly slept at all. Then one night she was awakened by shrill squeaking. She rushed into the room where the hamster cage was kept, and gasped. The door of the cage was open! She had been so tired the night

Now Chinese hamsters are successfully bred in many laboratories.

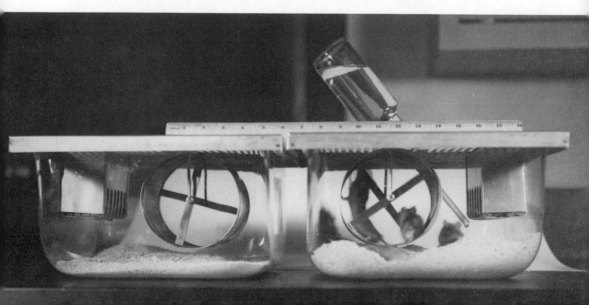

Hamsters are quick to take advantage of an open cage door.

before, she had forgotten to lock the cage. Now there were hamsters scurrying all over the floor. Mrs. Aharoni pounced, scooped up four of the little hamsters, and popped them into the cage. But the other six were already gone. They had gnawed several holes in the bottom of the wall and disappeared. Now she could hear them moving about, somewhere under the floor.

The next day the Aharonis thought about calling in a carpenter to take up the floorboards. But what if the hamsters had already tunneled through into the space under the other rooms? They couldn't tear up the whole house looking for the missing hamsters. So that night

14

the Aharonis set up a hamster watch. They spread papers on the floor and placed bits of bread and cucumber on them as bait. Then they settled down for a fitful doze. In the middle of the night, hungry hamsters came up out of their holes to search for food. The rattling of the papers as they scurried across them worked as an alarm. The Aharonis leaped up. Professor Aharoni snatched up wads of cotton and stuffed them into the holes in the wall, while his wife grabbed for the nearest hamster. After a few nights of this, they had caught five of the missing hamsters. (They never did find the last one.)

After this experience, Professor Aharoni decided to take the golden hamsters to the laboratory at the university. He turned them over to the supervisor of the animal department, who put them in a roomy cage with walls of steel wire and a floor made of a thick wooden plank. That was a mistake. The next morning, the horrified supervisor discovered that the hamsters had chewed a hole through the wooden floor of their cage, and five of them had escaped.

The remaining golden hamsters were quickly transferred to all-metal cages. They settled down in their new surroundings, and about four months after they were first dug out of their burrow in Syria, a young female gave birth to the first litter of golden hamsters ever born in captivity. Her young grew quickly, and soon there was a thriving colony of golden hamsters at the university. Dr. Adler found that they were indeed good research animals for studying kala-azar—just as good as the gray hamsters he had hoped to get. And the golden hamsters were so easy to raise that he thought they would be good for other laboratory studies, too. He sent some of his extra golden hamsters to scientists in France and England. Others were sent to India and Egypt. Finally, in 1938, some golden hamsters were sent to scientists working for the United States Public Health Service at Carville, Louisiana.

In laboratories around the world, hamsters lived and multiplied. The scientists who raised them noticed that these little animals quickly became tame and friendly. They didn't take much room and they were very clean. They would make ideal pets, especially for people who lived in the city. Some of the scientists took extra hamsters home as pets for their children. Pet dealers learned about the new animals from Syria and began to breed them. Suddenly hamsters were the hottest new pet craze in years.

Before the Second World War, only a handful of scientists had ever heard of golden hamsters. But now millions of people in the United States and other countries around the world keep these small rodents as pets. And nearly all the millions of hamsters now living in laboratories, schools, and homes are descended from the original litter that Professor Aharoni brought back from a burrow near Aleppo in 1930.

A WELL-EARNED NAME

The name "hamster" comes from a German word, *hamstern,* which means "to hoard." In Central Europe, in fact, a person who is greedy or selfish is often called a "hamster."

Hamsters in the wilds are real hoarders. They live mainly on fruits, vegetables, and seeds. Often they catch small rodents, lizards, or young birds as well. During the summer season, when food is plentiful, the hamster gathers as much as it can. It does not stop when it is no longer hungry. It stuffs seed after seed into the pouches in its cheeks. (A hamster was once observed fitting forty-two soybeans into its cheek pouches.) Its cheeks puff out

Hamsters can pack a surprising amount of food into their cheek pouches.

until it looks as though it is suffering from a bad case of mumps. When it has packed away every bit of food it can carry, the hamster takes its booty to its underground burrow and hoards it away in food storage chambers, connected to its sleeping chambers by tunnels.

The large hamsters that live in Europe are often a serious pest in farmlands. As much as a hundred pounds of potatoes and grain has been found in a single hamster's burrow. In China, hungry peasants would often dig into hamster burrows and take their stored grain for food.

WHAT IS A HAMSTER?

Hamsters belong to a group of rodents. These are small mammals, who share one main trait in common: a constant need to gnaw on things. Rodents' front teeth continue to grow as long as they live. Their constant gnawing helps to keep these front teeth worn down to sharp-cutting chisels. If you have ever chipped a front tooth, you must wish that people's front teeth kept on growing. But there can be some disadvantages. If a rodent—for example, a rat or a hamster in a cage—is given only soft foods and does not have a chance to gnaw, its teeth will grow so long that it cannot eat or even close its mouth.

There are more than two thousand different kinds of rodents. You probably know some of them very well. Rats and mice are rodents. So are squirrels, chipmunks,

Typical rodent teeth.

and prairie dogs. Beavers are rodents who use their sharp front teeth to cut down trees and build dams and lodges in ponds and streams. Porcupines, whose sharp quills protect them from enemies, are also rodents.

Among the rodents, the hamsters' closest relatives are

Rodents all—the hamster is just about the same size as the guinea pig's baby.

the various kinds of rats and mice, as well as muskrats and lemmings. Porcupines, squirrels, chipmunks, and prairie dogs are not as closely related to hamsters.

When the word "hamster" is mentioned, the average person in the United States thinks of a golden hamster. But there are actually a number of kinds of hamsters found in different parts of the world, of different sizes and colors, and somewhat different habits. They belong to four main groups: the common or European hamster, the golden or Syrian hamster, the gray hamster, and the dwarf hamster.

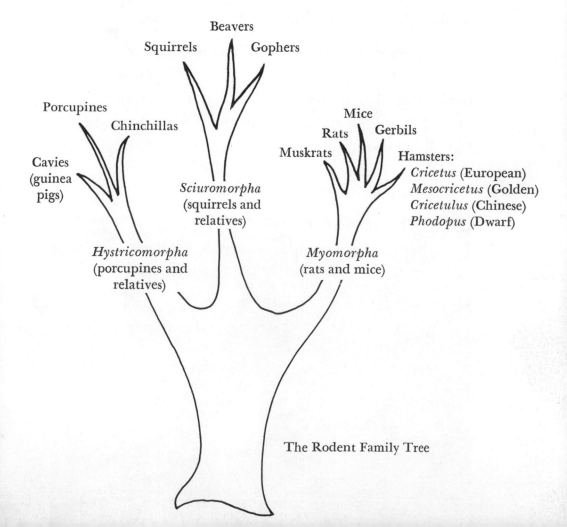

Beavers

Squirrels Gophers

Porcupines

Chinchillas

Mice

Rats Gerbils

Muskrats

Cavies
(guinea
pigs)

Hamsters:
Cricetus (European)
Mesocricetus (Golden)
Cricetulus (Chinese)
Phodopus (Dwarf)

Sciuromorpha
(squirrels and
relatives)

Hystricomorpha
(porcupines and
relatives)

Myomorpha
(rats and mice)

The Rodent Family Tree

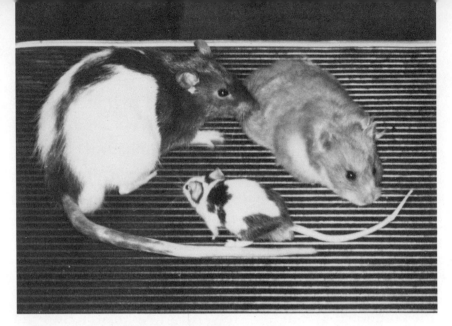

Larger than a mouse, but smaller than a rat.

GOLDEN HAMSTERS

A golden hamster is a chunky little rodent, larger than a mouse and smaller than a rat. But it is plumper than these sleek rodent relatives, and its skin is very loose-fitting. A golden hamster does not have a long slender tail like a rat or mouse; its tail is short and stubby. When

Not much of a tail.

it stands up on its hind legs to look or sniff around, some people think it looks like a little golden bear. But probably a golden hamster looks most like a cross between a large mouse and a very small guinea pig.

All the golden hamsters that live wild in Eastern Europe, Asia Minor, and Iran look alike. Their fur is a rich reddish gold, with whitish underparts, black markings on the head and cheeks, and a broad band of dark fur across the chest. Their eyes are black, and their ears are dark-colored and almost hairless.

Characteristics like fur color and eye color are inherited in hamsters, just as they are in other animals. (People also inherit their hair color, eye color, and skin color.) Like other animals—and people—wild hamsters tend to vary a bit. Perhaps one has an unusually long nose, while another has a very short nose. Perhaps one hamster has fur that is a bit lighter than usual. Pet breeders watch for animals that are a bit different, with a trait that seems desirable. They breed such animals, and they select those of their young that are carrying the traits they want to establish. For example, the original golden hamsters had long, pointed, ratlike heads. Pet breeders have bred hamsters for shorter heads and have produced new types that many people think are much cuter.

Pet breeders also watch for another kind of hereditary change, one that scientists call a mutation. Once in a while, a baby is born that is very different from its parents—not just a little bit different. A baby golden hamster may be born that has spotted fur, or light cream-colored fur, or pure white fur all over its body. Perhaps it has red eyes instead of black eyes. If this different hamster can pass its changed trait on to its own babies, then the change is a mutation, a change in the chemicals of heredity that parents pass on to their children.

Barely a few decades have passed since pet breeders began to work with golden hamsters. This would be far too short a time to try to follow hereditary changes in humans. People usually do not begin having children of their own until they are twenty or more. And they do not have many children in their whole lifetime. But a female golden hamster is ready to mate when she is only about two months old. In just sixteen days, her babies are born—perhaps a dozen of them at a time. She can go

Time and breeding have brought color variations: here, an original golden, a cream, and a black-eared albino.

on having litters every month or so until she is about a year old. And meanwhile, her babies grow up and can have litters of their own. So even in a few decades, hamster breeders have had many, many generations of golden hamsters to work with—literally millions of animals. Among these hamsters they have found and bred some interesting mutations. Today you can find many of them on sale in pet shops.

There are albino hamsters, with pure white fur and ruby-red eyes. (These hamsters are lacking the dark-colored pigment that normally gives color to skin, hair, and eyes—not only of hamsters, but of other animals and people as well. Their eyes look red because you can see the blood flowing in tiny blood vessels. In dark-eyed hamsters, the red blood color is hidden by the dark pigment.) Another variation, the black-eared albino, has pure white fur and red eyes, but the skin of its ears is black.

Note the pale eyes of this albino hamster.

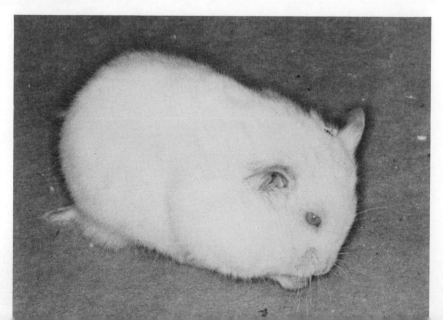

Piebald hamsters have a pattern of white spotting scattered over the body and a white blaze or streak on the face, running from the nose up to the top of the head. This was the first hamster mutation ever discovered. The amount of spotting varies from one animal to another, even in the same litter. Piebald hamsters are also called pandas, spotteds, and harlequins.

The cream mutation was discovered in Britain in 1948. This mutation makes the hamster's fur color lighter, producing a creamy apricot color. The amber gold mutation, producing a bright cinnamon-orange color, was discovered in the 1950's. So was the white band mutation, in which the hamster has a clearly marked white band around its middle.

Two white band hamsters and a golden.

Pink woolly—the first long-haired mutation.

Other mutations change the kind of fur. Woolly pink hamsters have curly pinkish fur. Other variations have been produced by crossing a hamster with one mutation with a hamster with a different mutation—for instance, cream panda. (But such combinations do not breed true. A pair of cream panda hamsters will give birth to litters that include some cream hamsters and some piebald hamsters.)

LIFE IN THE WILDS

Golden hamsters in the wilds usually live in dry places— among sand dunes, on steppes, and on the edges of deserts. Each hamster digs a burrow for itself, with a long tunnel entrance, a sleeping chamber, and several storerooms. Hamsters do not get along very well with each other. As soon as they are old enough to leave their mother—about three or four weeks after they are born—they go off to make their own homes. Males and females get together during the breeding season, in the summer. But they do not stay together after mating.

Golden hamsters usually spend the day curled up in their burrows, sound asleep. They are nocturnal animals, active mainly at night. After the sun goes down, they come out of their burrows and waddle quickly along on their short legs, with tiny hairy-soled feet. A hamster's short legs make it look awkward when it walks, but its sharp-clawed feet are good for digging. The powerful muscles of its hind legs permit it to crawl both forward and backward in the narrow tunnels of its burrow.

As the hamster scurries about picking up seeds and other bits of food, it packs them away in its cheek pouches. Soon the sides of its head are bulging out. It pauses every now and then to sniff and listen—for there are often enemies about that would consider a hamster a tasty meal. Hawks and owls may swoop down to snatch up an unwary hamster. Weasels and foxes hunt them, too. Snakes may even slither down into their burrows after them. But the hamster is not an easy prey. If it is attacked, it will fight back furiously, defending itself with its sharp teeth. If it is alert and lucky, it will make

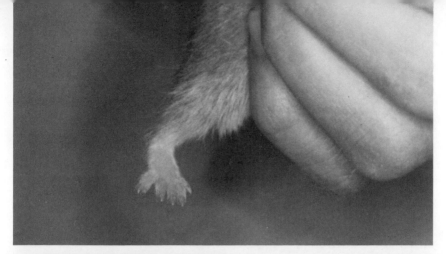

Four-toed feet with a tiny stub of a thumb.

it back safely to its burrow. There it unloads its booty by pushing on its cheek pouches with its front paws.

In the autumn, as the days grow shorter and there is a chill in the air, hamsters seem driven to even more activity. They make trip after trip through the fields, gathering grains and other foods and storing them away in their underground burrows. By the time winter comes, and there is no more food to be found, each golden hamster may have from thirty to sixty pounds of grain laid away. As the temperature drops, the hamster curls up in its burrow and stops moving. At first it seems to be going to sleep. But this is far deeper than any normal sleep. This is the winter sleep of hibernation. The hamster's heart slows down, from four hundred beats a minute to only four. It takes a breath only twice a minute. Its body temperature falls until it seems nearly as cold as its surroundings. It looks dead! If you shouted at it, or shined a light on it, it would not wake up.

In the state of hibernation, the hamster is conserving energy. Running around and keeping its body warm uses up a great deal of energy. Even breathing at its normal rate uses up energy. But when all the normal processes in its body are slowed down, a hibernating hamster can go for long periods of time without having to eat. It cannot go without food for a whole winter, though. Some hibernating animals sleep the whole winter through. Their bodies form thick layers of fat in the fall, and this fat provides all the energy they need. Woodchucks, for example, go to bed in the fall very fat and wake up in the spring very thin. But hamsters do not form layers of fat. Instead, the hamster wakes up from time to time during the winter. It nibbles some of the food that it has stored away, and then it goes back to sleep again. It will not wake up completely until the temperature rises in the spring.

COMMON HAMSTERS

Common hamsters can stand more moisture than golden hamsters. They are often found living in plowed fields or among farmers' crops. Some even live along river banks and swim with ease. When a common hamster swims, it fills its cheek pouches with air, so that they act like a pair of water wings.

The European hamster has black fur on its underparts.

Common hamsters are much larger than golden hamsters, about the size of a guinea pig. Their fur color is rather unusual. Most animals, like the golden hamster, have darker fur on their backs and whitish fur on their underparts. But the common hamster is light brown above and black below, with white patches on its sides. This black-bellied hamster, as it is sometimes called, is found through much of Europe and part of Asia, from Belgium to Lake Baikal in Siberia.

Like the golden hamster, the common hamster is a nocturnal animal, although it sometimes comes out of its burrow in the daytime. In the summer it digs a short, shallow burrow, with a sleeping chamber and another chamber for storing grain. As winter approaches, it digs a larger, deeper burrow. The winter burrow has not only a nesting chamber, but also several storerooms. One may be filled with grain, another with potatoes,

The common or European hamster is the largest of all the hamsters.

another with carrots or other roots, and another with nuts. In addition, a hamster burrow usually has a "bathroom" chamber—for the common hamster, like the golden hamster, is a very clean animal. It does not like to soil its sleeping nest or food stores. The entrances to the burrow are usually marked by mounds of earth that the hamster dug out, and perhaps some spilled grains. There may be one main entrance and several other entrances in a circle around it. But when the winter temperatures fall below 45° or so, the hamster blocks up all the entrances to its burrow, curls up in a ball in its nest, and goes to sleep. Like the golden hamster, it will spend the winter sleeping, waking now and then to eat from its food stores.

Common hamsters live mainly on cereal grains, although they also eat various fruits, roots, and green leaves. Often they vary their diet with frogs and lizards, as well as small rodents and nestling birds. Insect grubs are also a treat for them. But they eat and store away so much grain that farmers regard them as serious pests.

Common hamsters will fight with teeth and claws if they are attacked by a predator such as a fox or weasel. In fact, they are such courageous fighters that, if one is cornered, it will not hesitate to attack even a dog or a man. If a hamster is in danger when its cheek pouches are puffed out with food it has gathered, it has another, rather peculiar means of defense. It blows out the contents of its cheek pouches at its enemy. The food flies out with such force that the pointed ends of the seeds may sting the enemy painfully, causing it to take to its heels.

The common hamster's best defense in the struggle for survival is not its teeth or claws, or even its cheek pouches. It is its ability to breed. Like golden hamsters, common hamsters have from six to twelve young at a time, sometimes up to twenty. Their babies are born nineteen to twenty days after mating—a little longer than the golden hamsters' sixteen days. But it is still a short enough time for a mother hamster to have two or three or even more litters during the breeding season.

GRAY HAMSTERS

The hamster most familiar to people living in Asia is the gray hamster. There are a number of different species of gray hamsters, found from Greece and Bulgaria to the Altai Mountains at the border of Outer Mongolia. These hamsters are smaller than golden hamsters, from three to eight inches long. Their tails are the longest of any of the hamsters—up to four inches long. Their fur is a mousy gray above, with white underparts.

During the spring and summer, gray hamsters can be seen scurrying about both night and day. But in the winter they are completely nocturnal. They are aggressive little animals. If a gray hamster is attacked by a predator, such as a mink or ermine, it will immediately

The gray or Chinese hamster.

turn on its back and get ready to bite and slash with its sharp teeth and claws. Like other hamsters, gray hamsters normally live alone. But in the mating season, the males visit the burrows of the females and may stay with them for about ten days.

In Turkey and other countries of the Near East, gray hamsters are sometimes called "house-haunting hamsters." They are often found living in people's houses, like house mice. These regions have real house mice, too, but mice and hamsters are rarely found in the same houses. The gray hamsters move into clean, newly built houses, while mice prefer older, run-down houses.

A Chinese hamster street circus.

In China, children catch wild gray hamsters ("Chinese hamsters") and keep them as pets. Sometimes these little rodents have been trained to do various tricks and acrobatics and have been exhibited in street circuses.

DWARF HAMSTERS

The last group of wild hamsters is the tiny dwarf hamsters, who live in Siberia, Manchuria, and northern China. They are only two to four inches long, plus a short little tail. They are lighter in color than the gray hamsters—grayish or buff above and white below.

Dwarf hamsters are often found living among pikas, small relatives of the rabbits and hares. Pikas live in burrows among rock piles and they cut and gather grasses and twigs to make huge haystacks. Dwarf hamsters live peacefully among the pikas, sharing their burrows and paths.

Dwarf hamsters are the most timid of all the hamster species. They are much less aggressive than gray hamsters and do not defend themselves when they are attacked. Their natural gentleness and clean habits make these tiny hamsters charming pets, but they are not very well known outside China and the U.S.S.R.

COUSINS OR BROTHERS?

Scientists have wondered how closely the different kinds of hamsters are related. They have noticed that golden hamsters are found just about where the ranges of the common and gray hamsters overlap. And the size of the golden hamster is just about midway between the large common hamsters and the small gray hamsters. (The scientific name for the common hamster, *Cricetus,* comes from the word used for these animals in Czecho-slovakia and Poland, *kreček*. Scientists call the golden hamster *Mesocricetus* and the gray hamster *Cricetulus*. *Meso-* means "medium" or "middle," while *-ulus* means "little." So the common hamster is "hamster," the golden hamster is "middle-sized hamster," and the gray hamster is "little hamster.") In addition, the golden hamster usually has eighteen nipples, while both the common hamster and the gray hamster have only eight.

Some scientists have thought that this is more than just a coincidence. They have suggested that the first golden hamsters may have been the children of matings between common hamsters and gray hamsters.

There is some support for this idea in the science of genetics, the study of heredity. Scientists have found that the information of heredity—what determines whether a person has blue eyes or brown or green, and whether a hamster has brown fur or gray fur or golden fur, a long tail or a short one—is carried in chemicals. A complete set of these chemicals of heredity is found in every one of the trillions of tiny cells that form the body. They are grouped into structures called chromosomes. Each kind of animal or plant has a set of chromosomes that looks just like the set of any other member of its species. The garden pea, for example, has a set of 14 chromosomes, while a human being has 46 chromosomes in each of its cells. Scientists can actually see these chromosomes and count them under a microscope.

They have found that chromosomes occur in pairs. One chromosome in each pair is nearly identical to the other.

The common hamster has a set of 22 chromosomes, 11 pairs. So does the gray hamster. But these two sets of chromosomes carry somewhat different information, and they look a bit different under a microscope. (It is as though you had two necklaces of 22 beads each, one red and the other blue. Each necklace has the same number of beads, but they don't "match.")

When two animals mate, each of them passes on exactly half of its chromosome set to each of its children. A mother hamster, for example, provides each of her babies with 11 chromosomes, one of each chromosome pair in her set. Each baby gets 11 more chromosomes from its father, so that it ends up with the usual 22. But what if the mother were a common hamster, and the

A new mutation. The fur is long and silky on the hindquarters.

father a gray hamster? The babies would have 22 chromosomes, but the two halves of the set would not "match"—they would not pair up properly. As the tiny single cell that starts the life of each animal divided again and again, and more information was needed as the heart and lungs and head and feet started to form, things might start to go wrong. Very likely the growing baby would die even before it was born. And if it did manage to grow up into some sort of hamster-looking creature, it might not be able to have children of its own. This is what usually happens in the rare cases when animals of two different species mate. Once in a while, mixed-breed young are born and survive, for example, when a horse and a donkey are mated. (But a mule—their offspring—is sterile and cannot have young of its own.)

Yet sometimes an unusual thing happens. As the first tiny cell begins to grow, the set of chromosomes doubles. Normally the cell would then split in half, and each half would get one complete set of chromosomes. But sometimes the cell does not split until the chromosome set has doubled again. Now each cell of the new baby-to-be will have twice the usual number of chromosomes. This happens rather often in plants. Some varieties of wheat and other important crops actually have two or even three or four times as many chromosomes as their close relatives. It does not happen very often in animals. But just suppose something like that happened when a common hamster mated with a gray hamster. The babies

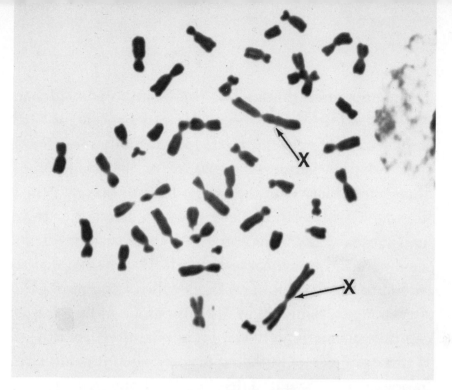

The 44 chromosomes of the golden hamster *(Mesocricetus auratus)* and the 22 chromosomes of the Chinese hamster *(Cricetulus griseus)*. The first set is shown as it appears when a single cell is photographed under high magnification. The second set was made from the same kind of photograph by cutting out the individual chromosomes and sorting them according to size and shape. The 22 chromosomes make 11 pairs.

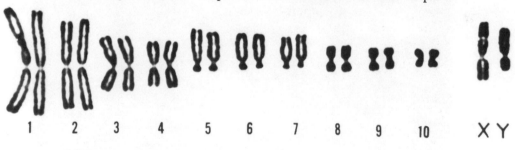

1   2   3   4   5   6   7   8   9   10   X Y

would have a complete matching set of 22 common hamster chromosomes *and* another complete matching set of 22 gray hamster chromosomes—a total of 44 altogether (22 pairs). Imagine how excited scientists were when they discovered that the golden hamster has a set of exactly 44 chromosomes!

Some scientists think all of this is just a coincidence. And indeed, they have since found other species of hamsters with different numbers of chromosomes. Some species of gray hamsters have 20, 26, or 30 chromosomes. Some close relatives of the Syrian hamster have 42 chromosomes, while others have only 38. And the dwarf hamsters have 28 chromosomes. All these varieties do not seem to fit into the theory very well. Hamster specialists intend to try to combine the sex cells of common hamsters and gray hamsters in the laboratory and see if they can breed something like a golden hamster from them. If this can be done in the laboratory, then it could have happened in the wild. The scientists hope that such experiments will some day answer the question once and for all.

Hamsters as Pets

Are you looking for a pet who is tame and friendly, clean and easy to care for, and doesn't take much room? Then perhaps you'd like to join the millions of people who have a hamster as a pet.

CHOOSING A HAMSTER

One of your friends may have a hamster who has recently had a litter. If so, he may be glad to give you a hamster or two. If you don't know anyone with a hamster to give away, you will want to buy one at a pet shop. Nearly every pet shop that stocks small animals carries hamsters these days. They are not very expensive

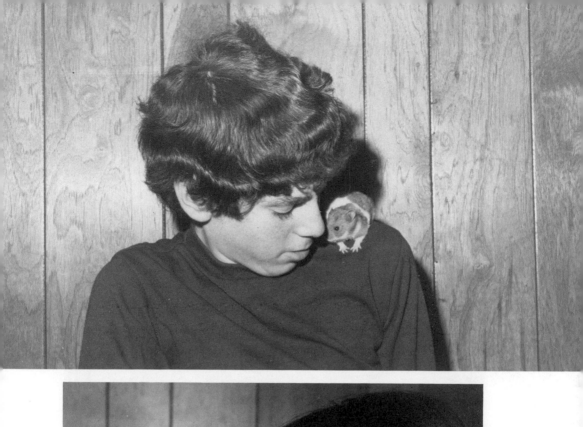

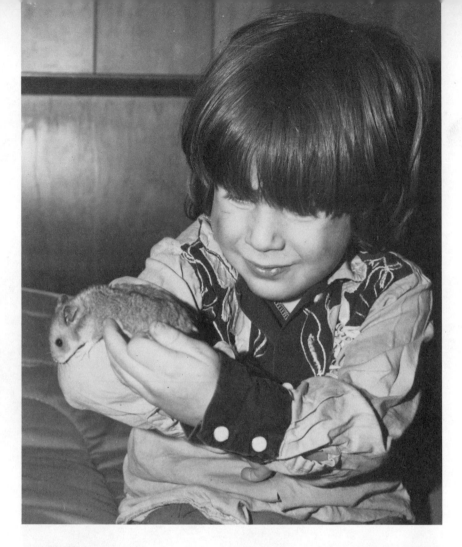

—a little more than a mouse, but less than guinea pigs, rabbits, cats, dogs, and almost any other animal you might want to keep as a pet. Often the pet shop will have quite a variety of hamsters to choose from—the original golden kind, plus various mutants and cross-breeds, such as cream, cinnamon, piebald, albino, and pink woolly. (The rarer kinds, such as pink woolly, may cost more.)

What kind of hamster would be best for you? If you

want to try breeding hamsters and are looking for some interesting results, you might take one or more of the mutants. But there are a few things you should remember. Scientists and pet breeders have found that some of the mutant strains are not as strong as the ordinary golden hamsters. Piebalds and ruby-eye mutants usually grow more slowly and stay smaller all their lives. Often mothers of these kinds have fewer babies in a litter, and many of the young die before they are fully grown. They are also much more nervous than other hamsters, and more likely to bite people who handle them and to fight with other hamsters. Cream hamsters, on the other hand, are usually very good-natured and calm, and less active and aggressive than the original golden kind. Albino hamsters may have poor eyesight. (Of course, no hamsters have really good eyesight. Like other nocturnal animals, they depend more on their senses of smell and hearing.)

Whether you are getting a hamster free or buying one at a pet shop, you should look at it carefully before you make your final choice. Are its eyes bright and its fur smooth and shiny? Are its underparts dry? (Wetness around the tail probably means the hamster has been having diarrhea. You might be able to cure it by feeding it a good diet and keeping its cage clean and dry, but why start out with problems?) A runny nose or watery eyes are also signs of poor health.

Don't just look at the hamster in its cage. Have your

How does the hamster act when it is out on the pet shop counter?

friend or the pet salesman take it out. How does it act when it is being handled? A hamster that has been handled gently and often will be tame and friendly and will seem to enjoy being picked up and patted. If it tries to bite, it may not have been tamed yet—this often happens when hamsters are raised in large colonies and not handled very much.

When the hamster is placed in a strange place, like the counter in the pet shop, how does it act? Does it run about, sniffing and exploring curiously? Or does it just huddle in one place, looking sick and frightened? Try offering it a tidbit. Move very slowly, so that you won't startle it. If it seems friendly and interested, you can try picking it up. You can close your hand around it very slowly and gently, so that its whole body is cradled in your hand. Or you can slide your two hands together, palms up, and cup it inside.

48

The best age to get a new hamster is about five to eight weeks old. At that age it is already weaned and old enough to be tamed and trained easily. (Very young hamsters are usually extremely shy.) But it is not old enough to have picked up bad habits. You can tell something about a hamster's age by looking at its ears. In young hamsters, the insides of the ears are covered with tiny white hairs. As the hamster grows, these hairs gradually disappear. An old hamster's ears are bare and shiny.

How many hamsters should you get? Some animals are normally so sociable that it is really not fair to them to keep only one. Guinea pigs and rabbits, for example, are happiest when they have a friend of their own kind to keep them company. But hamsters are rather solitary animals. In fact, they really do not like other hamsters very much, and they may fight viciously if two of them are kept together. (One may even kill the other!) So you

A litter of young hamsters, about five weeks old, ready to go to new homes.

need not feel guilty if you'd prefer to have just one hamster as a pet.

Of course, if you want to breed hamsters, you will need two, a male and a female. In fact, you might start with a male and two or even three females. (Hamsters do not choose mates for life, as some animals do. A male hamster will be perfectly happy to mate with two, three, or even more females.) It is not too hard to tell the difference between male and female hamsters. The male's testicles, right at the base of his tail, give the rear of his body a long, tapering shape, like a triangle. A female is much shorter and more rounded. If you hold the hamster on its back in the palm of your hand, you can see the male's penis about a quarter to half an inch from the vent. The outer opening of the female's sex organs, the vulva, is much closer to the vent. And from about ten days old, the female's nipples appear as two rows of dots along her belly.

Sexing a hamster: the male is on the left, the female on the right.

If you get more than one hamster, and if you plan to breed them, you must be prepared to buy or make a cage for each of them.

HOUSING

Some animals can be housed quite nicely in wood-framed cages. We have even kept guinea pigs in an ordinary cardboard box. And of course, some pets, such as cats and dogs, do not need a cage at all, but can safely be allowed the run of the house. You can't let a hamster run around free in a house. It will quickly make a pest of itself, and may do a lot of damage. It is a rodent, and like its rodent relatives, it has a constant need to gnaw. In the wilds, hamsters gnaw on hard seeds and nuts. They use their teeth to tear up leaves and plant fibers to line their nests. In a house, a hamster may chew on the legs of your furniture. One of us has a very early memory of his mother scolding him because his hamsters got loose and chewed up the fringe of her bedspread. Years later, we had a chance to find out how a parent feels when something like that happens. Our children came running. "Come quick! Tom is missing!" They had been playing with Tom, their pet hamster, on the sofa, a foam rubber lounge. Now they couldn't find him. We looked all over the living room, under the sofa pillows, on the floor in corners, behind the bookcase. No Tom. Suddenly we noticed something peculiar. It

Hamsters are always chewing on things.

was snowing under the sofa! At least, it looked like snow. A shower of fine white flakes was falling steadily to the floor. We quickly found the culprit. Tom, investigating the sofa, had discovered a small opening at the back of the mattress where the two zippers of the slipcover met. He slipped inside and quickly chewed out a hamster-sized hollow in the foam rubber. It was fortunate that we caught him when we did, before he had a chance to do something worse—like chewing on the electric wires!

So you must keep your hamster in a cage. You can't use a cardboard box, or even a wooden cage, for it will chew its way right out. A hamster cage should be a sturdy structure, made of metal. (You can use a wood frame if you cover the inside of it with wire mesh and paint it with a nontoxic paint to discourage gnawing.)

Hamster cages—get the biggest one you can.

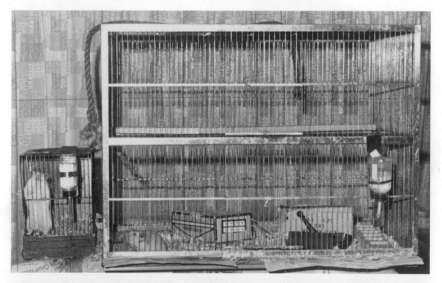

Pet shops and department stores usually carry cages that are good for hamsters. A metal cage with a slide-out bottom (for easy cleaning) is best. If you are handy with tools, you can also build a cage yourself. Any simple design will do nicely, as long as you provide for several things. At least one of the walls should be wire mesh, both to provide some climbing exercise for your hamster and to allow for air circulation so the cage does not become too damp. You will need a good-sized door so

that you can take your hamster in and out, feed it, and clean its cage. You can either cut a door in one of the walls, or hinge the top so that it lifts up. The bottom of the cage should be lined with a sheet of metal that can be taken out for cleaning. (You can get or cut a cookie sheet to fit.)

Some people use an old fish tank as a hamster cage. If you do, it is a good idea to replace one glass wall with wire mesh. And be sure to put a wire mesh cover on top, fastened securely.

A very simple cage can be made with two deep baking tins, either round or oblong, and a piece of wire mesh. Roll the mesh into a cylinder or oblong shape just the right size to fit snugly into one of the tins. Be sure to allow a couple of inches of overlap, and fasten the seam securely with wire. Set the mesh body of the cage into one tin and fit the other on top as a lid, and you are all set. (It is a good idea to keep a weight on top, so that the hamster can't just push up the lid and leave.)

If your cage has a latch, make sure that it closes tightly. At night, while you are sleeping, your hamster will be awake looking for things to do. It will bite on anything it can get its teeth around, and if the latch on its cage door is loose, it may be able to work it loose. If the cage has a pull-out tray on the bottom, you should be especially careful to push it in completely. If you leave enough space for the hamster to get a nose or a paw in, it may be able to push the drawer out far enough to get the rest of itself through.

An exercise wheel is good for running in . . .

or on!

Give your hamster as roomy a cage as you can. You should allow at least one square foot of floor space for a hamster; a cage 24″ by 18″ by 12″ high would be even better. Then you could furnish the cage with an exercise wheel, which you can get at any pet shop. You will find

A new idea in hamster exercisers . . .

and one you can make yourself.

that your hamster enjoys running on the wheel and may keep it up for an hour at a time. The exercise is good for the hamster, too, and keeps it from getting sluggish and bad tempered. If your cage is too small for an exercise wheel to fit comfortably, you can keep it outside the cage and take your hamster out for daily exercise periods.

Your hamster's cage should be supplied with a water jar or bottle. If you use a small jar or can for water, be sure to wire it solidly to the wall of the cage. Otherwise the hamster may knock it over and wet the inside of its cage. Golden hamsters live in very dry places in the wilds, and their descendants who live in homes and laboratories can't stand much moisture either. If its cage stays wet, your hamster may get sick and even die. An open water jar can be a danger in another way when a mother hamster is raising a brood of young. After the little hamsters begin to crawl around and explore their cage, one of them may get into the water jar accidentally and drown.

For these reasons, people who have hamsters or other small pets use a hanging water bottle instead of an open jar. You can get one in a pet shop, or you can make one of your own. You will need a small bottle, a cork or rubber stopper to fit it, with a hole in the center, and a piece of bent glass tubing. Fit the tubing into the stopper, fill the bottle with water, and hang it upside down on the outside of the cage, with the tubing extending into the cage through one of the holes in the wire

This kind of water dispenser won't get dirty or tip over.

mesh. It might seem as though the water would just run out and wet the cage. But it is held in by air pressure. The hamster licks drops of water from the end of the tube when it is thirsty. This kind of water bottle can be refilled easily without opening the cage. It should be rinsed out with fresh water each day.

You might also have a feeding dish. But many hamster owners don't feel this is necessary, since the hamster

Snug in a nest of shredded newspaper.

usually packs the food into its cheek pouches and moves it to another part of the cage anyway.

You should supply your hamster with some hard sticks to chew on, and perhaps a ham or beef bone. These will help to keep its ever-growing teeth filed down to just the right length.

The bottom of a hamster cage should be covered with a layer of cedar chips, straw, or some other absorbent material. Ordinary newspaper will do nicely. The hamster will enjoy ripping it up into fine shreds. Don't use pieces of old wool blankets or other cloth to line the cage. They will quickly get sopping wet. And the hamster may eat bits of wool, which can disagree with it.

You will find that your hamster quickly rearranges its

cage to suit itself. It will take some of the straw or shavings or paper strips and make a cozy nest in one corner. In fact, if you supply a nesting box, your hamster will be happy with it. (A wide can turned on its side can be used.) The hamster will leave its droppings all together in another part of the cage, away from the nest. Another corner of the cage, usually the one farthest from the nest, will be used for urination. You will find that your hamster always urinates in the same place. The shavings in that spot will get wet quickly and should be replaced every day. The rest of the cage need only be cleaned once a week.

You can put your hamster in a large glass jar for safe-keeping while you are cleaning out its cage. Take everything out and wash down the inside of the cage with a disinfectant cleaner. Be sure the cage is dry before you put new shavings down. You will find that the bedding from the hamster's nest is still fairly clean. Put most of it back, so that its cage will still seem like home. You will also find a hoard of extra food that it has been saving. Remove anything that is rotting, but be sure to put some of the stored food back where you found it. Otherwise, the hamster will be very upset when it gets back in its cage and will run around looking for its missing food stores.

If you follow this very simple cleaning schedule, you will find that a hamster is a very clean pet, and it and its home are almost completely odorless. In fact, some

A can or jar is good for temporary safekeeping while the hamster's cage is being cleaned.

hamster owners take advantage of their pet's clean habits to make cage cleaning even easier. After the hamster has chosen its corner for urination, the owner puts a large, widemouthed glass jar there. (A peanut butter jar would probably be just right.) Whenever the hamster wants to urinate, it just walks into the jar and does it there. It is a simple matter to lift out the jar once a day and wash it thoroughly.

Because hamsters are clean and just about odorless, you can keep your hamster cage anywhere that is convenient. But we suggest that you place a wide tray or pan under it if you are going to keep it in a bedroom or living room. Hamsters often rearrange their bedding, and shredded paper and shavings tend to fall out through the holes in the wire mesh. Our sons used to keep two hamster cages on their chest of drawers. Because they were sometimes a bit lazy about closing their drawers completely, they were always having to pick bits of shredded newspaper out of their clean underwear and pajamas.

Never keep a hamster cage in the sun. Hamsters are nocturnal animals, and bright sunlight may be painful for their eyes. Their ancestors were used to spending the sunlit hours hidden deep underground, and pet hamsters, too, need a place to hide from the daylight.

Hamster cages should not be kept outdoors, either, or in an unheated shed. If the temperature in the room drops below 45°, your hamster will hibernate. Its body will be cold and rigid, and you may think it is dead! (But it will slowly revive if you warm it gently in your hands and feed it warm milk from a medicine dropper.) Newborn hamsters cannot stand a temperature below 55°.

Another thing to guard against is allowing wild rodents or other household pests to get into your hamster's cage. They may be attracted by its food stores, but they can spread diseases and parasites.

FEEDING

Some animals, such as horses and cows, eat only plant food. Others, such as cats and dogs, eat mainly meat. But humans, pigs, and most rodents can eat almost anything. Hamsters are no exception. Although they eat mainly grains in the wild, they also feed on insect grubs, birds' eggs, and other animal foods when they can get them.

Some people feed their pet hamsters table scraps. These may be good for an occasional treat, but often they do not provide the balanced diet your hamster needs to keep it in the best of health. Pet shops and supermarkets sell a prepared food for hamsters that contains all the vitamins, minerals, and other nutrients they need. It comes in the form of little dry pellets. (If you run out of hamster food, you can substitute dog biscuits for a while.) It is especially good to feed hamsters mainly dry food because of their habit of storing food away.

Good foods for hamsters: fresh greens . . .

sunflower seeds, and hamster pellets or dog biscuits.

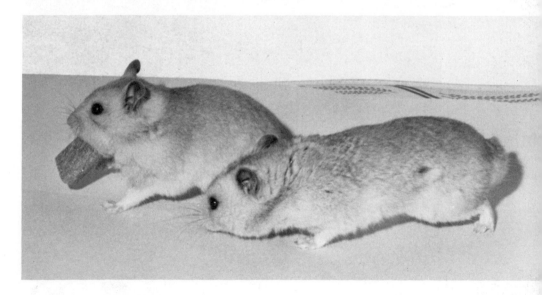

When you place a day's supply of food in the cage, your hamster will usually load as much as it can carry into its cheek pouches and scurry away to deposit the food in its special hideaway. Then it will come back for another load. It will visit its food stores from time to time to take a snack. A hamster holds a piece of food in its

65

A hamster washes itself like a cat.

forepaws, like a squirrel. When it has finished a meal, it brushes its face with its paws and washes itself all over like a cat.

A hamster eats about half an ounce of food a day. But you needn't worry about overfeeding it. If you give it too much food, it will eat only what it needs and store the rest away. In fact, hamster owners find that they can go away on a vacation and leave their pet alone for as much as a week. All they need do is leave it a big supply of dry food and hang an extra water bottle or two on the cage.

Although hamster food contains all the nourishment a hamster needs, it appreciates a little variety in its diet. Carrots and apple bits are good to give a hamster once or twice a week. Lettuce and grapes are good, too. But be sure to remove any extra fresh food before it has a chance to rot or get moldy. Spoiled food can make a hamster very sick. Sunflower seeds and peanuts are special treats. Your hamster may even appreciate some live food, such as ants, flies, or cockroaches. Milk is a very good food for hamsters, especially for pregnant hamsters and mothers nursing their young. You can serve a drink of milk in an upside-down bottle cap, or soak some whole wheat bread in milk. But be sure to remove any leftover milk before it turns sour. Some hamster owners solve this problem by giving their pets dry milk.

Don't try to feed your hamsters any acid fruits, like oranges or grapefruits. You should not feed them raw meat either, for this seems to make them more vicious toward other hamsters—they may even kill and eat each other. And evergreen needles should never be given to hamsters, either as food or as bedding. Their sharp points might irritate or even pierce the lining of the hamsters' cheek pouches.

FUN WITH HAMSTERS

When you first get your hamster, it may be very suspicious and wary, especially if it has been raised in a large colony and not handled very much. So first you will

A new hamster may be wary and suspicious . . .

but soon it will be walking right out onto your hand.

have to make friends with it. Let your hamster settle
down and get accustomed to its new cage at first. Make
sure there are no loud noises to frighten it, and let it
alone unless it seems eager to be friendly. It may take
a few days for it to rearrange its furnishings and settle

down comfortably. But there is no rush. Hamsters live for two or three years, so you will have plenty of time to play with it.

When your hamster seems happy and calm in its cage, you can start making friends. Put your hand in the cage slowly, offering it a tidbit such as a sunflower seed, a peanut, or a raisin. Hamsters are naturally curious little animals. Very likely it will walk up to sniff at your hand and investigate the tidbit you are holding. When it starts nibbling, you can try stroking it gently. (Remember not to make any sudden moves.) If it still seems calm, you can carefully close your hand around it and pick it up. You can hold it by the loose skin at the back of its neck, supporting its bottom with your other hand. Always be sure to give a hamster or any other small animal plenty of support when you are lifting or carrying it, so that it will feel secure. Gradually, as you pat it

This is a good one-hand grip for picking up a hamster.

Picking up a hamster: you can scoop it up in your cupped hands . . .

but watch out . . .

it won't stay still for long!

A hamster's skin is so loose that holding it by the scruff of the neck doesn't bother it at all.

and talk to it, your hamster will get to know you and become your friend.

Hamsters like to explore new places. If you put your hamster down on a tabletop or bed, it will run about from one end to another, sniffing and looking. Be careful when it is near the edge. Like many ground-dwelling animals, a hamster has no instinctive fear of falling. It may walk right off the edge of a table without realizing what might happen, and it could be seriously hurt in a fall.

A hamster has no natural fear of heights, but it may learn some caution.

If you put your arm down on the table next to a hamster, it will quickly learn to climb up your arm to perch on your shoulder. Its tiny feet are well adapted for climbing and grip your arm securely.

With patience, you can train a hamster to walk up your arm and perch on your shoulder.

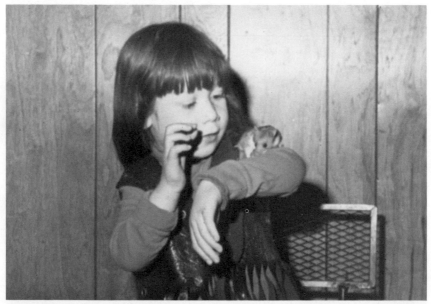

You can teach your hamster to do tricks. The key is using a reward, some tidbit the hamster especially likes, such as a peanut or a raisin. For example, if you place a raisin in your shirt pocket, your hamster may find it while it is climbing on your shoulder. Soon it will learn to climb up your arm and over your shoulder to get the raisin in your pocket. You can teach a hamster to stand up on its hind legs by holding a tidbit above its head and saying "Stand." In order to reach the tidbit, it will have

Stand up and beg!

to stand up. If you are patient and repeat the lessons enough times, it will eventually learn to stand up whenever you hold your hand over its head, whether you have a reward or not, or even when you just say "Stand." But be sure to reward it at least sometimes. Like people, hamsters get tired of working for nothing after a while and may forget a trick if they are never rewarded any more.

You can buy or make some toys and games for your hamster. An exercise wheel is one good one. Another is a ladder. You can make a ladder from two sticks and a coathanger. Cut the coathanger wire into pieces three inches long. Drill matching holes in the two sticks, an inch and a half apart. Then insert the wires into the holes to form the rungs of the ladder. A hamster will enjoy running up and down the ladder. You can make a sliding board by making two ladders and covering the lower half of one of them with smooth board. Wire the tops of the two ladders together securely so that they form an upside-down V and anchor the bottom. Another "must" for a hamster playground is a sandbox. Fill up a large grocery box with sand, surround it with newspapers, and let your hamster go to it. It will have a marvelous time, digging burrows as though it were back in its ancestral home in the Syrian desert. But be sure to keep an eye on the box, so your hamster doesn't escape.

It is fun to watch hamsters playing. Toys and

A ladder for climbing up . . .

and a slide for sliding down.

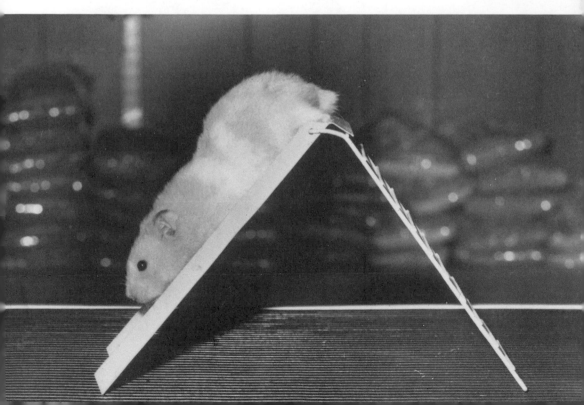

A homemade slide works just as well.

Sand to dig in—just like home!

The excitement of hamster racing . . .

sometimes the hamsters decide to change the rules.

Tightrope walking is fun, once a hamster gets the hang of it.

games are good for them too. Ladders, sliding boards, and wheels provide exercise, which helps to keep them in good health. And scientists have found that the brains of young animals who have been provided with games and toys and other interesting things to explore actually develop more than those of young animals who are kept in a plain cage with nothing interesting to do. By giving your hamster opportunities to play, you will actually be helping it to get smarter.

New experiences for hamsters—just the right size for toys.

Fun with simple things: a tissue role for a tunnel . . .

shavings for playing and chewing . . .

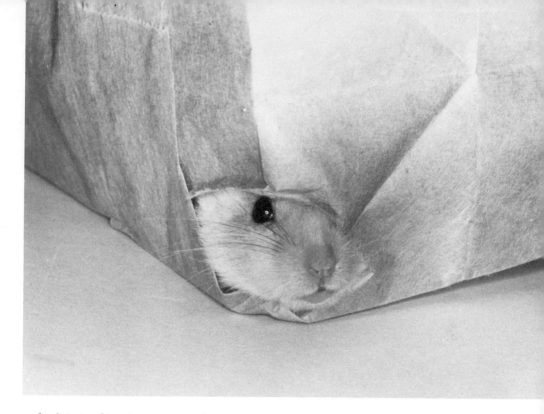

and a bag to chew its way out of.

Because hamsters are normally nocturnal animals, you will find your pet sleeping most of the day. It may wake up to play with you, but you will probably find it much livelier in the evening, after the sun has gone down. Never pick up a hamster suddenly when it is sleeping—if it is wakened suddenly, it will wake up fighting. As one hamster breeder says, it seems to be a general rule for a hamster to bite first and ask questions later.

You will find that two hamsters who would fight if they were put together in the same cage may get along quite well on neutral ground, such as a tabletop or your shoulder. For a hamster, its cage is not a cage—it is its home territory, and it will fight to defend it. Meeting another hamster outside, it does not have the same need to attack, and the two may sniff each other with interest. (Be prepared to grab them by the scruff of the neck and separate them if a fight does start, though.) In neutral territory, hamsters may also get along fairly well with other small pets, such as mice or guinea pigs. But don't put a hamster together with another animal in an enclosed place, such as a cage. One of our children once put a hamster and a mouse together in a large jar to see what would happen. The poor mouse immediately had a heart attack and died!

Some dogs have been trained to get along with pet hamsters. But generally we would recommend keeping hamsters strictly separate from dogs and cats. Hamsters look too much like rats or mice!

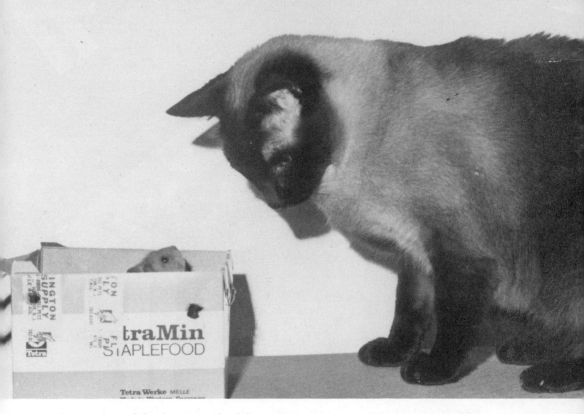

Some cats might be trusted with a pet hamster, but better not to take chances.

BREEDING HAMSTERS

One of the most enjoyable parts of keeping animal pets is watching them raise their families. There is something about watching tiny babies of any kind feeding and growing, playing and exploring and learning, that makes nearly everyone feel good inside.

Hamsters are just about the champion breeders among all the mammals (animals with hair who feed their young with milk). They can have more babies in a shorter time than even rats and mice, who are breeding specialists themselves. A mother rat or mouse carries her

83

The fun of raising hamster families.

babies for twenty-one days before they are born. But baby hamsters are born just sixteen days after their mother mated. A female hamster is ready to mate for the first time when she is about five weeks old (though pet breeders often recommend waiting until about three months for the first mating, so that the mother will be stronger and better able to raise her litter). She can mate again just four days after her babies are born (again, it is better for the mother to wait until the babies are weaned). And she has about six to twelve babies at a time, or even more. After a month or two, each daughter hamster could mate and start having litters of her own. They can go on having young until they are about a year old. Count them all up and imagine just how many hamsters there would be after a while. In a year, a single pair of hamsters could produce hundreds of thousands of children, grandchildren, and more distant descendants!

84

Fortunately, you will have some control over just how many baby hamsters you will have to cope with. After three or four weeks, when the babies are ready to leave their mother, you will separate the young males from the young females. Then, when they start to fight after a few weeks, you will want to put each hamster in a cage of its own. (Probably by that time you will be thinking about giving away some of the young hamsters or selling them to a pet shop.) So none of your hamsters will have a chance to have babies unless you want them to and purposely bring them together.

What is the best way to set up a hamster "romance"? After you have chosen the pair you want to breed, place each one in the other's cage for a little while (separately, *not* together!). That way, they will become familiar with each other's scent. For hamsters, with their poor eyesight, recognize other hamsters by their smell more than by their looks. Then put each hamster back in its own cage and put the two cages side by side. Leave them like that for a few days. The hamsters will be able to sniff at each other through the wire while each is still safe in his or her home territory, and they will get to know each other.

After this get-acquainted period, you can try a mating. Place the female in the male's cage and see what happens. It might be best to wear a glove when you do this. For if they start to fight, you will have to get them separated fast, before they hurt each other, and you don't want to get bitten in the process. *Never* place the male in the female's cage. That is her home territory, and she will fight to defend it, even if she might be interested in the male.

If it is so dangerous to put a male hamster in a female's cage, you might wonder why it is all right to put a female hamster in a male's cage. After all, that is *his* home territory. There are several reasons. First of all, female hamsters are usually more aggressive than males. (If there is a fight to the death between two of them, it is usually the male who is killed.) Secondly, females are much more fussy about their homes; often a male is not as tidy about his housekeeping and not as touchy about defending his nest. But most important, as soon as he is old enough (males mature about two weeks later than females), a male hamster is *always* ready to mate. A female, on the other hand, has what is called an estrus cycle. Every four days, tiny egg cells are released from her ovaries, the female sex glands. If she mates, these egg cells will join with sperm cells from the male and start the lives of baby hamsters. But this can happen only once in each cycle, on the evening of the first day. For the other three days of her estrus cycle, she will not be at all interested in mating.

As you can guess, if you want results, you should bring your two hamsters together in the evening. When you put the female down, the male will come up to her and sniff her eagerly. If she is ready to mate, she will suddenly stand rigid, with her tail up and her head held low. Then she and the male may run around the cage, stopping now and then to sniff each other. Finally the female will stop and allow the male to mount her.

If the female is not in the right part of her estrus cycle, she may attack the male. If she does, take her out quickly and try again the next evening. Eventually you should get some results. It is possible that the female may accept the male peacefully, even though she will not let him mount her. If this happens, it is all right to leave her in his cage and let them arrange their own mating. But take her out after a week and put her back in her own cage. She is probably pregnant by this time, and she will soon be getting short-tempered.

You will not have long to wait before you are sure that your hamster is pregnant, for her babies are due to

If the female is in the right part of her cycle, she will allow the male to mount her.

be born just a little more than two weeks after the mating. Soon her sides begin to bulge out, as the babies grow inside her. Be sure she gets plenty of nourishing food during this time, with an extra ration of milk. But leave her alone more than usual and clean her cage as little as possible. If you can, give a pregnant hamster a nesting box, about six inches by six inches, and provide her with plenty of bedding materials. Some cages, with a partition down the center, are ideal for a hamster about to have a litter. She can use the outer part as a "living

A breeding cage with a bedroom and a living room.

room" and the inner half (connected to the other by a doorway in the partition) as a nesting chamber. It is best to have a pregnant hamster's cage in a quiet place, where she will not be disturbed.

Some hamsters remain tame and friendly all during pregnancy. But others get increasingly short-tempered and may bite if you try to handle them. If you need to clean a pregnant hamster's cage, you can lure her out by placing a tidbit in the bottom of a large can, turning it on its side, and placing it next to the open door of her cage. Her curiosity will prompt her to walk into the can. Then you can turn it upright and take care of the cage. Work quickly and keep an eye on the can. For the hamster will quickly flip over inside and soon be standing on her hind legs, peering over the edge.

Almost exactly sixteen days after the hamster mated, you will hear squeaking from the nest. You won't see anything because the new babies are buried in a small mountain of nesting materials. If you could see them, you would be surprised. The babies do not look like hamsters. Their skin is bare and pink, their eyes and ears are sealed tight shut, and they have flat little pug-nosed faces. In a few days their bodies become covered with a fine coat of fur. Baby hamsters of the original golden variety at first have mousy-colored fur, but it changes to reddish golden as they grow.

You will be dying to get a look at the new babies. But resist the temptation! Hamsters are extremely nervous mothers. If they become upset, they may refuse to care for their babies, or even kill and eat them. Continue to give the mother hamster plenty of food, for now her body is making milk to feed her babies. But don't clean her cage or try to look at the babies for at least a week. If you do touch one of the babies, touch all of them. When you touch them, you leave the smell of your hand on their bodies. If just one of the babies smells different from the others, the mother hamster may kill it.

Indeed, mother hamsters, like many other species of animals, recognize their babies by smell rather than sight. We once got a mother hamster to accept a baby

Newborn baby hamsters in their nest.

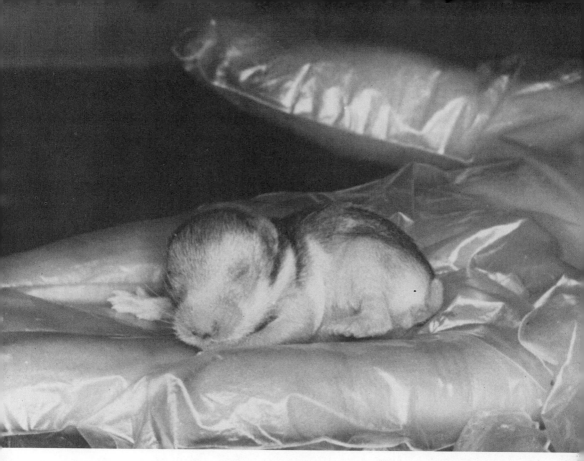

If you must handle baby hamsters, using plastic gloves may help to keep them from picking up your smell.

mouse as a foster child by rubbing carbolated vaseline on the mother's nose. By the time her sense of smell was back to normal, the baby mouse had picked up the smell of the baby hamsters in the litter, and she raised it like one of her own.

When the baby hamsters are about a week old, they are beginning to crawl around the nest and starting to nibble at their mother's solid food. But their eyes are still sealed tight shut. They will not open until the fourteenth or fifteenth day.

One day old.

Watch the hamsters grow. At first they don't look like much, but soon their fur grows and their eyes open. (Each square is ½ inch.)

Three days old.

Seven days old.

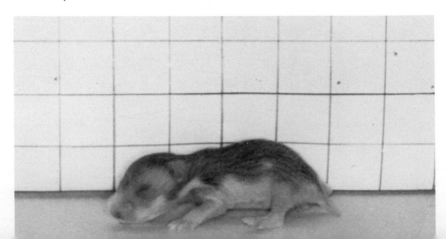

Twelve days old.

Sixteen days old.

By eighteen to twenty-one days, the young hamsters are ready to be weaned. They are eating enough food on their own to do without their mother's milk. Now is the time to separate them from their mother, especially if she seems to be getting nervous. They have sharp little teeth now, and when they try to nurse, they may bite their mother's nipples. We once made the mistake of leaving a litter of young hamsters with their mother too long. Suddenly we noticed that there seemed to be one baby hamster missing. The next day there was one less, and the next day still another was gone. At that point we realized what was happening and gave the little ones a cage of their own. After that, no more disappeared.

Breeding hamsters has an element of fun that few other animals can provide. Because hamsters are still relatively new as pet and laboratory animals, only a handful of mutations have been discovered and studied. Mutations do not happen very often. But in any litter you might find a hamster of a type that no one has ever seen before. (Later in the chapter you will read about how we lost our chance for scientific fame.)

It is important to keep good records of your hamster

A new mutation. At five weeks, this hamster looked like an ordinary cinnamon (a lighter colored variation of the golden). The long fur on her hindquarters grew out later. (Her littermates are shown in the picture on page 49.)

breeding. For each mating, make a note of such facts as the names of the parents, their general appearance (cream, spotted, albino, and so forth), any special characteristics (for example, very nervous or very calm), their ages, and the date of the mating. Then you will add the date of birth, the number in the litter, the kind of care the mother gives them, and descriptions of the babies.

After some experience, you will be able to figure out for yourself some laws of heredity. For example, some characteristics seem to be dominant—if a purebred parent has the characteristic, then all its children will show the same characteristic, no matter what kind of mate it had. The wild-type golden color is a dominant. Most of the hamster mutations that have been discovered so far, on the other hand, are recessive characteristics. This means that they will show up in a baby hamster only if it has inherited them from both parents. The cream mutation is recessive; so are the albino and piebald characteristics. If you mate a purebred golden hamster with the typical golden coat with a cream hamster, all the babies will have the golden coat. But if you mate one of those babies with another cream hamster, about half of the new litter will have golden coats and half will have cream coats.

The white band is one mutation that seems to be a dominant. The children of a white band hamster may have a white band of fur around their middles even if

The white band mutation is inherited, and the amount of white varies.

one parent was a purebred golden. But when the white band characteristic is inherited from both parents, the babies have much more white fur. (Scientists usually call a characteristic like this an incomplete dominant—it shows a little when it is inherited from only one parent and more when it is inherited from both.)

The laws of heredity that you can learn from your hamsters work for other animals, too—cats, dogs, horses, and even people. So by studying hamsters you can learn more about the world around you.

YOUR HAMSTER'S HEALTH

If you feed your hamster a balanced diet and keep its cage clean and dry, you should not have to worry much about health problems. But hamsters, like people, do get sick or injured sometimes, and it is reassuring to know what to do about it.

If you are keeping several hamsters together, you may occasionally find a hamster who has been bitten by one of its cagemates. If the bite is in a place it can reach with its tongue, it will lick the wound clean, and it will probably get better without any help from you. If the wound is in a place that the hamster can't lick, dab it with a mild antiseptic such as merthiolate. But don't try to bandage it—the hamster will only rub and scratch at the bandage until it comes off, and it may make the wound worse in the process. And never leave a wounded hamster in the same cage with other hamsters. They may attack it.

Hamsters can catch colds, just as people do. In fact, they can catch colds from people, so never let anyone with a cold play with your hamster. If your hamster does catch a cold, it will suffer from sniffles and a runny nose just as you do, and it may lose its appetite. Put its cage in a warm, dry place, out of drafts, and give the hamster plenty of fresh water and a few drops of cod liver oil on a piece of bread. Clean out its cage thoroughly and put in fresh litter. Do this again after it is better, so that it will not get infected all over again. If it is living with other hamsters, separate them as soon as it shows signs of illness. A wide-mouthed jar with litter on the bottom and a wire mesh cover can be used as a temporary "isolation ward."

Another problem hamsters share with people is tooth decay. Check your hamster's teeth every now and then for signs of decay. (Wear gloves when you do it.) More milk in its diet may help to keep its teeth healthier. Overgrown front teeth can prevent a hamster from chewing its food properly, and it may grow weak and ill. Be sure to provide your hamster with hard chewing materials, such as nuts and twigs, to avoid this problem.

Keep an eye on your hamster's droppings as an indication of its health. If they seem very hard and dry, it probably is not getting enough water or fresh fruits and vegetables. Loose, watery droppings mean that the

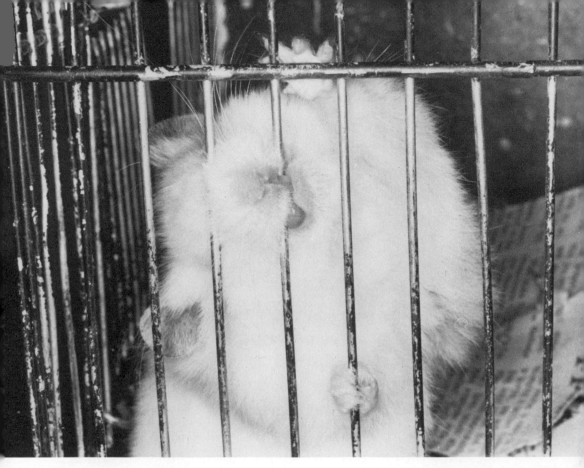

Give your hamster plenty of chewing materials. Chewing on the wire of the cage may break a tooth.

hamster is getting too much fresh food, and you should cut back to dry food for a while. (But your hamster should still have all the water it wants to drink.)

A serious disease that sometimes spreads through hamster colonies is called "wet tail," because diarrhea makes the hamster's tail region wet and irritated. Scientists still are not entirely sure what causes wet tail—germs, or perhaps something lacking in the diet. Sometimes brewer's yeast is helpful in treating it.

A coat with a moth-eaten appearance and skin irritations may mean your hamster is suffering from mites. It may also catch fleas from other household pets or wild rodents. You can get rid of these parasites with one of the commercial sprays. Always use a preparation made for cats, not dogs, since hamsters lick their fur just as cats do.

A WORD OF WARNING

Whenever a new kind of animal is brought into a country as a pet or laboratory animal, or even an exhibit in a zoo, public health and agriculture officials are very concerned about what might happen if some of them escaped. Hamsters are clever little escape artists, and people who have hamsters as pets may sometimes be tempted to turn them loose if they do not want to keep them any more. But hamsters on the loose have the potential for becoming quite a nuisance.

In cities, wild hamsters could cause the same sort of problems as rats and mice, living in holes in the walls and spoiling food and chewing on things. They could even cause fires by chewing on electric cables. And how they can multiply! In one case reported in England, six golden hamsters escaped from a pet shop. A year later, someone in the neighborhood reported a suspected rat infestation. People from the health service came out and put down traps. They did not catch any rats, but they caught fifty-two golden hamsters.

Don't let your hamster become a "public enemy"! Keep it in a securely fastened cage. . .

a loose door can quickly lead to a hamster on the loose.

In farm areas, hamsters might become agricultural pests, just as they often are in their native lands. In most of the United States and Europe, the climate is not warm and dry enough for hamsters to do well, and native predators such as snakes, hawks, owls, and foxes could probably keep any escaped hamsters under control. But parts of Australia and New Zealand have an ideal climate for golden hamsters. So these two countries do not permit anyone to bring golden hamsters in for any reason—not for pets, or even for scientific research.

The United States does not ban hamsters. (It is much too late for that, even if anyone wanted to.) But the U.S. Department of Agriculture has issued a warning:

> Breeders of hamsters are cautioned to prevent the escape of any of these animals. Such release under favorable conditions might establish the hamster in the wild and thereby create a serious rodent problem, since they are destructive to growing crops, gardens, and other agricultural enterprises. Purchasers should be aware of the danger of escapes, and make every effort to prevent the establishment of a wild colony.

A number of years ago, we had an interesting experience with hamsters, which taught us a great deal about how they live and how they might become pests. We were living in the city at the time, and we had a yearly problem with cockroaches. Normally we didn't have any. But each fall, as the weather turned cold, they would suddenly appear. Apparently the excess roach population from other houses in the neighborhood had spent a pleasant summer out in the backyards, and now they were seeking a warm shelter for the winter. (We even caught some squeezing in under the door.) Unfortunately, generations of city dwellers have been using every insecticide spray and powder known against generations of cockroaches. Such sprays usually kill most of the pests, but a few resistant ones survive and breed resistant offspring. As a result, the cockroaches that invaded our house each fall were big and healthy and were not at all affected by the sprays we tried. The only really effective method of controlling them that we

could think of was to prowl around the house at three
o'clock in the morning, turning on the lights suddenly
and squashing any cockroach we found, until the last
invader was gone. Needless to say, this was a rather dis-
agreeable thing to have to do, and one year we decided
to try a bit of applied ecology.

At the time, we had three hamsters: Tom, a cream-
colored male (the one who ate a hole in our foam rubber
lounge), and two cream-colored females. We had read

Tom and his mates were all cream-colored hamsters.

that hamsters eat insects, so we decided to turn ours loose in the cellar, to work on the latest cockroach immigrants. The cellar had solid cinder block walls and a cement floor, so we figured that the hamsters wouldn't be able to go anywhere and we could just gather them up when the last roaches had disappeared.

Other people have also tried experiments in ecology, and they have often found that things did not turn out exactly the way they expected—for the relationships of animals to one another and to their environment are usually much more complicated than anyone realizes.

At first everything seemed to be going nicely. The hamsters settled down in their roomy new home and would come running eagerly when we came down to give them some food and water. Our first shock came when we turned on the cellar light one night and discovered two fat cockroaches contentedly feeding from the same dish as the hamsters. Apparently hamsters just don't bother to eat cockroaches when there is something better available. While we were thinking about what to do next—perhaps cut down on their food a bit—we suddenly noticed a small pile of fresh dirt next to the foot of the steps. The previous owner of the house had apparently put in a new flight of steps, with a slightly steeper pitch than the old ones. Two narrow slits in the cement floor remained to mark the position of the old stair supports. We hadn't really noticed them before, but now we saw that they had been filled with hard-packed dirt.

Each one was only about an inch wide by three or four inches long. But that was enough for the hamsters. They had dug a neat hole at the end of one slit, and now they apparently had a burrow under the cellar floor. While we were digesting that new piece of information, we made another discovery. The bag of hamster pellets was empty. The hamsters had apparently found a way to climb up to the shelf, gnawed a hole in the bottom of the bag, and removed the food, pellet by pellet. Since we bought our hamster food by the fifty-pound bag, they were now independent!

Meanwhile, we had been noticing signs that the little colony was thriving. Little hamsters were sometimes seen scurrying across the floor, and after a while there were big hamsters, middle-sized hamsters, and new little hamsters. They were all cream-colored, of course, like their parents and grandparents.

Our hamster colony in the cellar gave us some interesting experiences, even though it didn't solve the cockroach problem. There was a small brown mouse living in the cellar at that time, too. He wasn't a wild mouse. The year before, we had been breeding mice. Apparently one of the mice had slipped out without our realizing it. We discovered him about six months later, sleeping in one of the open cages on the rack by the wall. We never did figure out what he was eating, but since he was an only one and a cute, cheeky little thing, we never bothered to do anything about him. When the hamsters moved in, he warily kept his distance. But feeding time proved an irresistible temptation. He would creep quietly toward the feeding dish. Then one of the hamsters at the dish would notice him, turn around, and give him a look. The mouse would quickly dart away. But soon he would be back, waiting for an opportunity to dash in and snatch a bit of food. We watched this happen many times. The hamsters usually paid little attention to him unless he got too close, and they never actually chased him. (The little mouse eventually died of old age in his open cage.)

After a while, we decided enough was enough and tried to round up the hamsters. But, except for Tom, they were all wild. Then our problem was unexpectedly solved by accident. One day we happened to leave an empty plastic bucket in the middle of the cellar floor. The next day it had a hamster in it. We are not sure how the hamster climbed in (probably by boosting itself up on the handle). But once in, it couldn't climb back up the smooth sides of the bucket to get out again. We removed the hamster and put it in a cage. Out of curiosity, we left the bucket there. Sure enough, the next morning there was another hamster in it. For several weeks we collected a hamster from the bucket almost every morning. They were always cream-colored.

Then one day there was a pure white female in the bucket, with pink eyes. If we had only known! We recently read a scientific report on hamster genetics and found out that at the time of our discovery no pure albino hamsters had yet been identified, only black-eared albinos. If we had realized at the time how important our little white hamster might be, she could

An albino hamster packs its pouches, ready for a trip.

have been the parent of a whole new line of hamsters. But instead, we just tamed her and gave her away to one of the children in the neighborhood.

Our plastic bucket eventually collected all the hamsters in the cellar. At least, there came a day when no hamster appeared in the bucket, and we never saw one running loose again. We don't know for sure whether any of the colony ever tunneled under the foundation of the house and escaped into the world outside. We hope not.

Hamsters
in the Laboratory

In 1946, one of the leading experts on hamsters, Dr. Hulda Magalhaes, began to compile a list of all the articles on experiments with hamsters that had been published by scientists. In the years that followed, she traveled to libraries all over the United States and England, corresponded with hamster lovers all over the world, and, with the help of students and other scientists, revised the list over and over again. By 1963, her bibliography of work on the golden hamster totaled more than five *thousand* titles! And all this since 1930.

LEARNING ABOUT HAMSTERS

What do scientists who work with hamsters study? Many

Hamsters in the laboratory.

of them have simply studied hamsters—their habits,
their needs in food and housing and care, the diseases
they suffer from, and their heredity. The hamster has
presented an unusual opportunity for a generation of
scientists. It is not often that a brand-new research animal is discovered. Many wild animals do not turn out to
be good research animals at all. Some need some special
food. (The koalas of Australia, for example, eat only
eucalyptus leaves.) Some will not breed in captivity.
And some are so timid that they go into shock and die
immediately if they are captured. So it is not too often

that scientists have a chance to start from scratch with an animal they can breed in unlimited numbers and study thoroughly. Golden hamsters were first described back in 1839. But no one really knew anything much about these animals until Dr. Aharoni brought back the litter of them in 1930 and bred some of them successfully.

Hamsters make good research animals for many of the same reasons they make good pets. They are easy to raise and care for, do not take much room, are not smelly, and breed faster than any other mammal. Golden hamsters in the wild have a definite breeding season. But in the home and in the laboratory, they can breed all year round. (There may be somewhat fewer litters in the summer and winter, if the room is allowed to get too hot or cold.)

Actually, although scientists in the United States

study mainly golden hamsters, scientists in other parts
of the world often use other kinds of hamsters. In the
U.S.S.R., golden hamsters, Chinese hamsters, and even
the little dwarf hamsters are raised in laboratories and
used for scientific experiments.

DISEASE STUDIES

The first experiment ever tried with golden hamsters
was on the tropical disease kala-azar, caused by the bite

of a sand fly. Professor Aharoni had hoped that these little rodents would be a good animal for studying this disease, and indeed they turned out to be. Before 1930, kala-azar was nearly always fatal. But now, as a result of experiments with golden hamsters, effective treatments have been developed and can cure 90 percent of the cases.

Kala-azar is a disease caused by a microscopic parasite. Hamsters have also been used in studies of other microscopic parasites, as well as parasitic flatworms and roundworms. They have also played hosts to viruses in experimental studies of such diseases as poliomyelitis, canine distemper, mumps, equine encephalitis, influenza, and rabies, as well as viruses suspected of causing cancer.

Hamsters have become a favorite research animal in studies of cancer, a disease in which body cells "run wild" and grow uncontrollably. Their cheek pouches provide a convenient "living laboratory" in which the growth of tumors can be studied. If a hamster is anesthetized by an injection of a drug, the cheek pouch can be carefully turned inside out and tumor cells inserted under the thin lining membrane. This lining is nearly transparent, so that a scientist can easily watch the development of the tumor under it. The pouch is readily turned right-side-out again, without any damage or discomfort, and the hamster lives a normal life until the researcher is ready to look at the tumor again.

In other cancer experiments, the effects of cancer-causing chemicals are being tested on hamsters. In one series of studies, for example, Russian scientists are using dwarf hamsters to learn whether chemicals that cause mutations can also cause cancer.

Since scientists have been studying hamsters, some of these animals have developed such diseases as muscular dystrophy, gallstones, cirrhosis of the liver, and goiter. There is even a strain of Chinese hamsters, all of whom have a tendency to develop diabetes. (Medical experts believe that diabetes is inherited in humans, too.) So hamsters are now being used to study all these diseases, in the hope that what is learned can be applied to humans.

One disease for which hamsters have proved to be especially good experimental animals is dental caries, or tooth decay. Hamsters often have even more trouble with their teeth than people do. Researchers noticed that some hamster families seemed to have more cavities in their teeth than others. For a while they thought the condition was hereditary and tried to breed strains that were particularly sensitive or resistant to tooth decay. But then a whole litter of "resistant" hamsters came

Tooth decay. The hamster whose teeth are shown on the left was treated with bacteria and fed a diet high in sugar. Healthy hamster teeth are shown on the right.

down with cavities. In time it was discovered that tooth decay in hamsters was spread more like an epidemic of bacterial disease than a hereditary condition. A tooth decay-causing factor was found in the droppings of hamsters, and it was thought that it might actually be some kind of bacteria.

Experiments on germfree animals, born under sterile conditions and raised in special isolating chambers without contact with any germs at all, finally proved that bacteria do indeed cause tooth decay. (A diet with a lot of sugar helps too, by providing food for the bacteria.) Unfortunately, those experiments had to be conducted on rats. For so far no one has been able to raise germfree hamsters. Raising germfree animals requires complete control of many conditions, including a completely sterilized diet. Vitamins and other substances are then added, to replace those that are destroyed by sterilization. Apparently there is something needed in hamsters' diet that scientists have not discovered yet, for when baby hamsters are raised in a germfree chamber, they do not grow properly.

NUTRITION STUDIES

Many of the scientific studies of hamsters have dealt with their food requirements—their needs for the basic food substances such as proteins, carbohydrates, fats,

vitamins, and minerals—and with comparison of hamsters' food needs with those of other laboratory animals. Diets that help prevent tooth decay and gallstones in hamsters have been developed.

As a result of experiments on hamsters, food researchers are now on the trail of some new growth factors that have not yet been identified. One of them is apparently found in milk, which made hamsters grow better when it was added to the standard feed. Another growth substance seems to be found, curiously enough, in human saliva. Hamsters given a mixture of water and human saliva to drink grew faster than hamsters who drank plain water.

117

HIBERNATION AND LOW-TEMPERATURE STUDIES

Hamsters in the wilds are hibernating animals. So, as you might expect, they are one of the animals scientists are using to study the effects of low temperatures and what happens in an animal's body during hibernation. They have found, for example, that although a hamster's body temperature falls when it hibernates, it is still under control: it is always a few degrees above the temperature of the surroundings. Researchers have also studied the effects of hibernation on various chemicals in hamsters' blood and tried to determine what makes them start to hibernate and what makes them wake up.

But hamsters are really not very good hibernators. They wake up too easily, for one thing. (Even if they are not disturbed, they rarely sleep more than two or three days at a time.) And it is hard to get them to hibernate when the researcher wants them to. When the temperature is lowered, some hamsters begin to hibernate, some just act normal (perhaps a bit more sluggish than usual), and some die. (So you'd better not try any hibernation experiments on your pet hamster!)

MEMORY AND LEARNING

Like rats and mice, hamsters can be taught to run through mazes, making the correct choice at each turn. They can also learn to solve simple problems. (Sometimes they are too smart for comfort, on problems like how to get out of a cage.) So it is natural that scientists studying how the brain works in memory and learning have used hamsters in some of their experiments. In fact, hamsters played a key role in one of the "landmark" studies of memory research.

In early experiments, scientists had used flatworms. They trained the worms to make the correct choice in a very simple maze, shaped like a T. Then they chopped up the trained worms and fed them to flatworms that had never seen the maze. (Flatworms don't mind being cannibals.) When the cannibal worms were put in a T maze, they learned the correct choice much faster than ordinary worms did. Somehow the cannibal worms had seemed to gain the knowledge of the trained worms by eating them.

As you can imagine, reports of these experiments sparked a wave of excitement. Scientists in other laboratories began raising and training flatworms. But then some of them said they could not repeat the experiments. And other scientists claimed that flatworms couldn't even learn anything anyway. Experiments on smarter animals were needed—animals that everyone could agree were really learning and remembering.

Enter the hamster. In one series of experiments, hamsters were taught that whenever a light flashed, there would be food in their feeding box. Soon the trained hamsters would run to the feeding box as soon as the light flashed. Then chemicals from the hamsters' brains were injected into the bodies of rats. The rats had never seen either the light or the feeding box before. But as soon as the light flashed, the rats turned toward the feeding box. Somehow the brain chemicals from the hamsters transferred their memories to rats.

Once these experiments were successfully repeated, scientists were at last convinced that there are indeed "memory chemicals" in the brain. New theories of memory and learning are now being worked out, and some specific memory chemicals have even been isolated. For example, scientists are now studying a chemical that causes an animal to be afraid of the dark when it is injected.

You can conduct your own learning studies. How long will it take the hamster to learn to find its way through the maze? Record the time it takes and the number of mistakes it makes in each trial.

PARAPSYCHOLOGY

Hamsters are taking part in experiments in one of the most "far-out" frontiers of science: parapsychology. Many people have had experiences that are very hard to explain without assuming that some sort of ESP (extra-sensory perception) is operating. For example, have you ever suddenly thought of an old friend you hadn't seen in a long time—and then met him on the street or received a letter from him? Have you ever dreamed about something, and then had it actually happen to you? Scientists in various laboratories are now studying people who have experiences such as these. They are trying to observe such people under strict laboratory conditions. But there is a problem with studying ESP: usually a person who claims to be able to tell what is going to happen in the future, or to know what other people are thinking, cannot control his ability. In the laboratory, with scientists staring at him, his parapsychological abilities may not work. And many people who claim to have "psychic powers" are actually cheating. In fact, there has been so much trouble in getting repeatable results in experiments of this kind that many scientists do not believe that ESP exists at all.

So parapsychological researchers at the Foundation for Research on the Nature of Man in Durham, North Carolina, got an idea: instead of using people, who might cheat or "freeze up" in scientifically controlled experiments, they are studying ESP in animals. They

The setup for precognition experiments—can hamsters predict the future?

are trying to learn if hamsters and gerbils can foretell the future. They are studying this ability, which is called precognition, with a very simple setup. Electric wires are connected to a metal cage. A hamster is placed in the cage, and then a mild electric shock is delivered to either one side of the cage or the other. If the animal is in the side of the cage that receives the shock, it quickly jumps over to the other side. But strangely, the researchers find that often the hamsters are able to avoid getting any shock at all by jumping over to the other side of the cage just *before* the electric current arrives. Somehow they seem to know which side of the cage will be "safe." Yet even the researcher doesn't know in advance which side of the cage will receive any particular shock, because the process is controlled automatically. Somehow the hamsters seem able to predict the future!

From deadly diseases to the mysteries of the mind, studies of hamsters are continuing in many fields of scientific knowledge. Already the descendants of that one litter in the Syrian desert have helped to save uncounted human lives and to add to our knowledge of the world around us.

Index

Page numbers in italics indicate illustrations.